Celebrate Re

Honoring God by Making Repairs

The Journey Continues

PARTICIPANT'S GUIDE 7

John Baker is the founder of Celebrate Recovery®, a ministry started at Saddleback Church. It is estimated that over the last 25 years more than 1.5 million people have gone through this Christ-centered recovery program. There are currently over 27,000 churches that have weekly Celebrate Recovery meetings.

John has been on staff since Celebrate Recovery started. He has served as the Pastor of Membership, the Pastor of Ministries, and is currently the Pastor of Saddleback Church's Signature Ministries. He is also serving as one of the nine Elder Pastors at Saddleback. John is a nationally known speaker and trainer in helping churches start Celebrate Recovery ministries.

John's writing accomplishments include Celebrate Recovery's *The Journey Begins* Curriculum, *Life's Healing Choices*, the *Celebrate Recovery Study Bible* (general editor), and *The Landing* and *Celebration Place* (coauthor). John's newest books are *Your First Step to Celebrate Recovery* and *The Celebrate Recovery Devotional* (coauthor).

John and his wife Cheryl, the cofounder of Celebrate Recovery, have been married for more than four decades and have served together in Celebrate Recovery since the beginning. They have two adult children, Laura and Johnny, and five grandchildren.

Johnny Baker has been on staff at Celebrate Recovery since 2004 and has been the Pastor of Celebrate Recovery at Saddleback Church since 2012. As an adult child of an alcoholic who chose to become an alcoholic himself, Johnny is passionate about breaking the cycle of dysfunction in his family and helping other families find the tools that will lead to healing and openness. He knows that because of Jesus Christ, and by continuing to stay active in Celebrate Recovery, Maggie, Chloe, and Jimmy—his three children—will never see him drink. Johnny is a nationally recognized speaker, trainer, and teacher of Celebrate Recovery. He is a coauthor of the *Celebrate Recovery Daily Devotional*, *Celebration Place*, and *The Landing*, and is an associate editor of the *Celebrate Recovery Study Bible*. He has been married since 2000 to his wife Jeni, who serves alongside him in Celebrate Recovery.

Celebrate Recovery®

Honoring God by Making Repairs

PARTICIPANT'S GUIDE 7

The Journey Continues

NEW CURRICULUM!

A recovery program based on eight principles from the Beatitudes

JOHN BAKER & JOHNNY BAKER

FOREWORD BY RICK WARREN

ZONDERVAN®

ZONDERVAN

Honoring God by Making Repairs

This title is also available as a Zondervan ebook.

Requests for information should be addressed to:
Zondervan, *3900 Sparks Dr. SE, Grand Rapids, Michigan 49546*

ISBN 978-0-310-13150-2 (softcover)
ISBN 978-0-310-13151-9 (ebook)

Cover design: Brand Navigation
Cover photography: 123rf.com

First Printing May 2016 / Printed in the United States of America

Contents

Foreword

The best known ministry at Saddleback Church—that is going to last for easily 100, maybe 200 years—started when a guy, who was a drunk, came to me with a 13-page letter. And that ministry is called Celebrate Recovery®.

Now, let me just put this in perspective. This may be Saddleback's greatest contribution to the world. Over 20,000 people have completed the step studies at Saddleback's Celebrate Recovery. Over three and a half million people worldwide have gone through a Celebrate Recovery step study.

Right now, around the world, 27,000 churches are using Saddleback's ministry called Celebrate Recovery—27,000 churches! It is so successful that Celebrate Recovery is the official recovery program in 44 state and federal prison systems. It has been translated into 20 different languages.

Do you think John Baker, when he came to see me in my office many years ago and said, "I've got an idea for a ministry, Pastor Rick," imagined it would be affecting three and a half million people in 27,000 churches? No. You have no idea what God wants to do through you. You may have the next big ministry idea. You may have the next Celebrate Recovery dwelling in you—a ministry that could be started and reproduced to bless the whole world. One guy, out of his own pain, starts a ministry that now affects tens of thousands of churches and millions of people.

Rick Warren

(Excerpted from Pastor Warren's talk at Angel Stadium on Saddleback's 35th anniversary)

Introduction

So far in *The Journey Continues*, you have done some great work. You've taken a close look at any denial that may have snuck back into your life; you've also learned about what God's power and hope can do for you as well as committed to daily seek His will.

Then you completed another a spiritual inventory, listing all of the good and the bad that you've done and that's been done to you. Hopefully the questions in these participant's guides have taken you further down the road to recovery and helped you go deeper into identifying your issues and defects of character.

In this guide, *Honoring God by Making Repairs*, you will see how continuing to confess and admit your faults will ready you to experience more victories. Then you will be able to make any new or outstanding amends and offer the forgiveness to others that you have received from Christ through His grace.

As you begin this second to last study in *The Journey Continues*, we will be praying that God will be with you as you do your part to make repairs in your relationships.

John Baker
Johnny Baker

The Road to Recovery

Eight Principles Based on the Beatitudes

By Pastor Rick Warren

1. **R**ealize I'm not God. I admit that I am powerless to control my tendency to do the wrong thing and that my life is unmanageable. (Step 1)

   "Happy are those who know that they are spiritually poor."
   (Matthew 5:3)

2. **E**arnestly believe that God exists, that I matter to Him, and that He has the power to help me recover. (Step 2)

   "Happy are those who mourn, for they shall be comforted."
   (Matthew 5:4)

3. **C**onsciously choose to commit all my life and will to Christ's care and control. (Step 3)

   "Happy are the meek." (Matthew 5:5)

4. **O**penly examine and confess my faults to myself, to God, and to someone I trust. (Steps 4 and 5)

   "Happy are the pure in heart." (Matthew 5:8)

5. **V**oluntarily submit to any and all changes God wants to make in my life and humbly ask Him to remove my character defects. (Steps 6 and 7)

   "Happy are those whose greatest desire is to do what God requires." (Matthew 5:6)

6. **E**valuate all my relationships. Offer forgiveness to those who have hurt me and make amends for harm I've done to others when possible, except when to do so would harm them or others. (Steps 8 and 9)

   "Happy are the merciful." (Matthew 5:7)
   "Happy are the peacemakers." (Matthew 5:9)

7. **R**eserve a time with God for self-examination, Bible reading, and prayer in order to know God and His will for my life and to gain the power to follow His will. (Steps 10 and 11)

8. **Y**ield myself to God to be used to bring this Good News to others, both by my example and my words. (Step 12)

   "Happy are those who are persecuted because they do what God requires." (Matthew 5:10)

Twelve Steps and Their Biblical Comparisons*

1. We admitted we were powerless over our addictions and compulsive behaviors, that our lives had become unmanageable. I know that nothing good lives in me, that is, in my sinful nature.

   "For I know that good itself does not dwell in me, that is, in my sinful nature. For I have the desire to do what is good, but I cannot carry it out." (Romans 7:18)

2. We came to believe that a power greater than ourselves could restore us to sanity.

   "For it is God who works in you to will and to act in order to fulfill his good purpose." (Philippians 2:1)

3. We made a decision to turn our lives and our wills over to the care of God.

   "Therefore, I urge you, brothers and sisters, in view of God's mercy, to offer your bodies as a living sacrifice, holy and pleasing to God—this is your true and proper of worship." (Romans 12:1)

4. We made a searching and fearless moral inventory of ourselves.

   "Let us examine our ways and test them, and let us return to the Lord." (Lamentations 3:40)

5. We admitted to God, to ourselves, and to another human being the exact nature of our wrongs.

   "Therefore confess your sins to each other and pray for each other so that you may be healed." (James 5:16)

6. We were entirely ready to have God remove all these defects of character.

   "Humble yourselves before the Lord, and he will lift you up." (James 4:10)

7. We humbly asked Him to remove all our shortcomings.

"If we confess our sins, he is faithful and will forgive us our sins and purify us from all unrighteousness." (1 John 1:9)

8. We made a list of all persons we had harmed and became willing to make amends to them all.

"Do to others as you would have them do to you." (Luke 6:31)

9. We made direct amends to such people whenever possible, except when to do so would injure them or others.

"Therefore, if you are offering your gift at the altar and there remember that your brother or sister has something against you, leave your gift there in front of the altar. First go and be reconciled to them; then come and offer your gift." (Matthew 5:23–24)

10. We continued to take personal inventory and when we were wrong, promptly admitted it.

"So, if you think you are standing firm, be careful that you don't fall!" (1 Corinthians 10:12)

11. We sought through prayer and meditation to improve our conscious contact with God, praying only for knowledge of His will for us, and power to carry that out.

"Let the message of Christ dwell among you richly." (Colossians 3:16)

12. Having had a spiritual experience as the result of these steps, we try to carry this message to others and practice these principles in all our affairs.

"Brothers and sisters, if someone is caught in a sin, you who live by the Spirit should restore that person gently. But watch yourselves, or you also may be tempted." (Galatians 6:1)

* Throughout this material, you will notice several references to the Christ-centered 12 Steps. Our prayer is that Celebrate Recovery will create a bridge to the millions of people who are familiar with the secular 12 Steps (we acknowledge the use of some material from the 12 Suggested Steps of Alcoholics Anonymous) and in so doing, introduce them to the one and only true Higher Power, Jesus Christ. Once they begin that relationship, asking Christ into their hearts as Lord and Savior, true healing and recovery can begin!

Serenity Prayer

God, grant me the serenity
to accept the things I cannot change,
the courage to change the things I can,
and the wisdom to know the difference.
Living one day at a time,
enjoying one moment at a time;
accepting hardship as a pathway to peace;
taking, as Jesus did,
this sinful world as it is,
not as I would have it;
trusting that You will make all things right
if I surrender to Your will;
so that I may be reasonably happy in this life
and supremely happy with You forever in the next.
Amen.

Reinhold Niebuhr

Celebrate Recovery's Small Group Guidelines

The following five guidelines will ensure that your small group is a safe place. They need to be read at the beginning of every meeting.

1. Keep your sharing focused on your own thoughts and feelings. Limit your sharing to three to five minutes.
2. There is NO cross talk. Cross talk is when two individuals engage in conversation excluding all others. Each person is free to express his or her feelings without interruptions.
3. We are here to support one another, not "fix" another.
4. Anonymity and confidentiality are basic requirements. What is shared in the group stays in the group. The only exception is when someone threatens to injure themselves or others.
5. Offensive language has no place in a Christ-centered recovery group.

Lesson 12

Confess

Principle 4: Openly examine and confess my faults to myself, to God, and to someone I trust.

"Happy are the pure in heart." (Matthew 5:8)

Step 5: We admitted to God, to ourselves, and to another human being the exact nature of our wrongs.

"Therefore confess your sins to each other and pray for each other so that you may be healed." (James 5:16)

Please begin your time together by reading "The Fifth Step, Day 120" from the *Celebrate Recovery Daily Devotional.*

"We Admitted to God, to Ourselves"

"For all have sinned and fall short of the glory of God, and all are justified freely by his grace through the redemption that came by Christ Jesus." (Romans 3:23–24)

This passage tells us that we have all have missed the mark. We all have done things for which we need God's forgiveness. We're all in the same boat. We've all sinned. We've all made poor choices. We all have hurts, hang-ups, and habits, just in different areas and degrees.

God's forgiveness takes place invisibly. What actually happens when God forgives us? How does forgiveness work?

1. God forgives instantly.
2. God forgives freely.
3. He forgives completely.

The Bible says, "Therefore, there is now no condemnation for those who are in Christ Jesus" (Romans 8:1). How great it feels to live with no condemnation, to live with the knowledge that God loves us in spite of all our faults!"

"And to Someone I Trust"

God tells us that it is absolutely essential to share our moral inventory list with another person: "Admit your faults to one another and pray for each other so that you may be healed" (James 5:16).

How does this verse say we are healed? By admitting our faults to one another. Why can't we just admit our faults to God? Why must another person be involved? Because the root of our problems is relational. We lie to each other, deceive each other, and are dishonest with each other. We wear masks and pretend we have it together.

We deny our true feelings and play games largely because we believe, "If they really knew the truth about me, they wouldn't love me." We become more isolated than ever. We keep all of the junk of our past inside, and we get sick. There's a saying: We are only as sick as our secrets. The hurts, hang-ups, and habits that we try to hide end up making us sick, but "revealing your feelings is the beginning of healing."

When you risk HONESTY with another person, all of a sudden, a wonderful feeling of freedom comes into your life.

(Excerpted from Life's Healing Choices, *John Baker, © Howard Books 2013)*

CONFESS

C—Confess all our sins, both those of commission and omission

Confession means that we agree with God regarding our sins. Confession restores our fellowship. Remember, sins of *commission* are committed when we do the wrong thing, while sins of *omission* are committed when we know the right thing to do but choose not to do it.

James 4:17 clearly states what a sin of omission is: "If anyone, then, knows the good they ought to do and doesn't do it, it is sin for them."

"He who conceals his sins does not prosper, but whoever confesses and renounces them finds mercy." (Proverbs 28:13)

O—Obey God's direction and repent

We need to "own up" to the sins we discovered in our inventory.

"Therefore let us move beyond the elementary teachings about Christ and be taken forward to maturity, not laying again the foundation of repentance from acts that lead to death, and of faith in God." (Hebrews 6:1)

> *We cannot ask forgiveness over and over again for our sins, and then return to our sins, expecting God to forgive us. We must turn from our practice of sin as best we know how, and turn to Christ by faith as our Lord and Savior.*
>
> —Billy Graham

N—No more guilt!

We can restore our confidence and our relationships, and move on from our "rear-view mirror" way of living that keeps us looking back and second-guessing ourselves and others.

"Therefore, there is now no condemnation for those who are in Christ Jesus." (Romans 8:1)

<u>F—Face the truth</u>

To continue moving forward in our recoveries requires honesty!

"But whoever lives by the truth comes into the light, so that it may be seen plainly that what they have done has been done in the sight of God." (John 3:21)

<u>E—Ease the pain</u>

When we share our deepest secrets, we begin to divide the pain and the shame. The more often we share our story, the freer we become from our pasts. A healthy self-worth develops that is no longer based on the world's standards but on the truth of Jesus Christ!

"If we claim to be without sin, we deceive ourselves and the truth is not in us. If we confess our sins, he is faithful and just and will forgive us our sins and purify us from all unrighteousness." (1 John 1:8–9)

"When I kept silent, my bones wasted away through my groaning all day long. For day and night your hand was heavy on me; my strength was sapped as in the heat of summer. Then I acknowledged my sin to you and did not cover up my iniquity. I said, "I will confess my transgressions to the LORD." And you forgave the guilt of my sin." (Psalm 32:3–5)

<u>S—Stop the blame</u>

We cannot find peace and serenity if we continue to blame ourselves or others.

"How can you say to your brother, 'Let me take the speck out of your eye,' when all the time there is a plank in

your own eye? You hypocrite, first take the plank out of your own eye, and then you will see clearly to remove the speck from your brother's eye." (Matthew 7:4–5)

S—Start living in Christ's truth and love

To sum up the benefits of Principle 4 in one sentence, it would be this: In confession, we open our lives to the healing, reconciling, restoring, uplifting grace of Jesus Christ who loves us in spite of ourselves.

"Grace, mercy and peace from God the Father and from Jesus Christ, the Father's Son, will be with us in truth and love." (2 John 1:3)

Questions for Reflection and Discussion

"For all have sinned and fall short of the glory of God, and all are justified freely by his grace through the redemption that came by Christ Jesus." (Romans 3:23–24)

1. How do these verses apply to your life?

2. How have they affected your daily actions?

3. Tell about a sin of omission, a time when you knew the right thing to do but chose not to do it.

"Therefore, there is now no condemnation for those who are in Christ Jesus." (Romans 8:1)

4. What does this verse say about your past?

5. How has it affected your daily actions?

6. Take some time to examine your heart to see if you are inappropriately blaming anyone for mistakes you've made. List them below.

7. How did you feel after confessing your sins to God? Be specific.

8. How have your relationships improved since you started living God's truth in love?

"Grace, mercy and peace from God the Father and from Jesus Christ, the Father's Son, will be with us in truth and love." (2 John 1:3)

Prayer

Dear God, thank You for Your promise that if we confess, You will hear us and cleanse us, easing our pain and guilt that keeps us locked in the past. Thank You that You always love us, no matter what. In Jesus' name, amen.

Lesson 13

ADMIT

Principle 4: Openly examine and confess my faults to myself, to God, and to someone I trust.

"Happy are the pure in heart." (Matthew 5:8)

Step 5: We admitted to God, to ourselves, and to another human being the exact nature of our wrongs.

"Therefore confess your sins to each other and pray for each other so that you may be healed." (James 5:16)

Please begin your time together by reading "Feeling Alone, Day 115" from the *Celebrate Recovery Daily Devotional.*

Part of Principle 4 is sharing the full results of our moral inventory with at least one other person. For many of us, this process goes against what we have been taught. For the rest of us, there are certain things we don't mind sharing with others, but some things we want to keep to ourselves. In *The Journey Begins,* we looked at what we stand to lose and what we stand to gain when we follow God in this process.

Now we are going to remind ourselves of why this is so important. Some of us have been in recovery for a long time by now. You may even be a sponsor or a leader at Celebrate Recovery. After completing *The Journey Begins*, you may feel as if everyone expects you to have it all together. But remember what Step 5 says:

"We admitted to God, to ourselves, and to another human being the exact nature of our wrongs."

And the Bible tells us, "Therefore confess your sins to each other and pray for each other so that you may be healed" (James 5:16).

The process of admitting our faults to each other doesn't end once we've completed a step study. In fact, it is an ongoing process that leads to our healing. Let's look closely at James 5:16 to see why and how we should do this.

ADMIT

A—Accountability is necessary for healing

"Confess your sins to each other ... so that you may be *healed*."

Notice it doesn't say "so that you may be *forgiven*." That only happens when you turn your life to Christ and CONFESS your sins to God and turn away from them. Instead, it says *healed*. Part of finding the healing we are looking for comes from accountability.

D—Don't pretend you have it all together

"Confess *your sins* to each other ..."

You need *at least* one person with whom you are completely honest. The voice that tells you to keep it to yourself, to hide, and to convince people you are fine is a liar. Use the time you meet with your sponsor or accountability partner to be open and honest.

M—Make sure both people share

"Confess your sins to *each other* ..."

This process is a two-way street! This is not a time for one person to listen and have the answers while the other person shares. If you are reviewing your inventory—what some people refer to as "doing a 5th Step"—it makes sense for one person to do the talking and the other to mostly listen. However, this process of meeting together, sharing, and praying for each other should be an ongoing one. So make it a *mutual* time of sharing and prayer.

Everyone—whether a first-time visitor, a Celebrate Recovery leader, or a pastor—needs this kind of relationship or their recovery will stall.

I—Intercede for each other through prayer

" … and *pray for each other* … "

To intercede means to pray on behalf of another. When you meet together, pray for each other. You may have a few people you meet with regularly. In fact, that's a good idea. It might be face-to-face or over the phone, but instead of ending the conversation with, "I'll pray for you," take time to actually pray together. Then, throughout the week, lift up your accountability partner in prayer, asking God to give them the freedom they are looking for.

T—Tell others of the healing you have found

There is an important distinction to be made here: tell others of the healing *you* have found, but *do not* reveal the secrets that have been shared with you. What your accountability partners share with you is strictly confidential.

Definitely tell other people about the changes Jesus has been making in you through Celebrate Recovery. Don't keep it to yourself! Others need to know that change is possible. Look for ways to let them know you are changing.

"But he said to me, 'My grace is sufficient for you, for my power is made perfect in weakness.' Therefore I will boast all the more gladly about my weaknesses, so that Christ's power may rest on me." (2 Corinthians 12:9)

Questions for Reflection and Discussion

1. Who do you have in your life with whom you can be open and honest? (Remember, this person needs to be of the same gender.) How did you find this person?

2. Are you this kind of person for anyone else? Explain.

3. Share about a time an accountability partner helped you find healing.

4. How do you make sure you are completely honest with at least one other person? How do you fight the voice within that tells you complete honesty isn't safe?

5. What ways have you found to make sure this kind of sharing is a two-way street?

6. Share a few ways that praying for other people and having them pray for you has helped your recovery.

Prayer

Take some time to share some personal prayer needs with the group and then close.

> *Heavenly Father, thank You for the people in this group. Thank You for sending me people I can be open and honest with. Help us find freedom over our hurts, hang-ups, and habits. Please help us with the things we just shared, and help us pray for each other this week. Amen.*

Lesson 14

Ready

Principle 5: Voluntarily submit to every change God wants to make in my life and humbly ask Him to remove my character defects.

"Happy are those whose greatest desire is to do what God requires." (Matthew 5:6)

Step 6: We were entirely ready to have God remove all these defects of character.

"Humble yourselves before the Lord, and he will lift you up." (James 4:10)

Please begin your time together by reading "The Sixth Step, Day 150" from the *Celebrate Recovery Daily Devotional.*

In some recovery material, Step 6 (Principle 5) has been referred to as the step "that separates the men from the boys!" I would also like to add, "separates the women from the girls!"

One of the reasons that Principle 5 "separates the men from the boys"—or the "women from the girls"—is because it states that we are ready to "voluntarily submit to every change God wants to make in my life."

When we worked this principle in *The Journey Begins*, most of us were very willing to have certain character defects go away. The sooner the better! But let's face it, some defects were harder for us to give up.

So, in this lesson, we're going to take another look at those old defects of character that we may have held onto. Also, we're going to determine if we have developed any new character defects. Yes, if we've been lacking in working any part of our program, new defects of character have developed. That is especially true if we have not been going to meetings or talking to our sponsors regularly. Additionally, it's a fact that we can get so involved in sponsoring or serving others, we neglect our own recovery.

Let's look at the new acrostic for READY.

READY

R—Review and pray to see if we have allowed any old or new defects of character to enter our recovery

Use your latest inventory sheets (completed in *The Journey Continues*) and compare them to your inventory sheets from *The Journey Begins*. Notice if there are any similarities (i.e., old defects of character) on both sheets, or if new issues have begun since completing *The Journey Begins*.

"Let us examine our ways and test them, and let us return to the LORD." (Lamentations 3:40)

E—Establish a plan for how we are going to allow God to help us get rid of our new defects of character

We need to make sure we share this plan with our accountability partner/team and ask for their input and prayer.

"Do not those who plot evil go astray? But those who plan what is good find love and faithfulness." (Proverbs 14:22)

A—Accept the changes that God is asking to us make in our lives

Continuing to hold onto character defects is not doing us or anyone close to us any good! Change is hard, but it heals.

"But he gives us more grace. That is why Scripture says: 'God opposes the proud but shows favor to the humble.'" (James 4:6)

"Humble yourselves before the Lord, and he will lift you up." (James 4:10)

D—Do replace our character defects with positive alternatives

The best way to accomplish that is one word—serve. We will discuss how to start more healthy habits in Lesson 19 of *The Journey Continues.*

"When an impure spirit comes out of a person, it goes through arid places seeking rest and does not find it. Then it says, 'I will return to the house I left.' When it arrives, it finds the house unoccupied, swept clean and put in order. Then it goes and takes with it seven other spirits more wicked than itself, and they go in and live there. And the final condition of that person is worse than the first. That is how it will be with this wicked generation." (Matthew 12:43–45)

Y—Yield to God's direction to continue growing spiritually

We will get out of *The Journey Continues* what we are willing to put into it.

"Test yourselves to make sure you are solid in the faith. Don't drift along taking everything for granted. Give yourselves regular checkups." (2 Corinthians 13:5, MSG)

"Anyone who lives on milk, being still an infant, is not acquainted with the teaching about righteousness. But solid food is for the mature, who by constant use have trained themselves to distinguish good from evil." (Hebrews 5:13–14)

Questions for Reflection and Discussion

1. Since completing *The Journey Begins*, have you allowed any of your defects of character to return? If so, list them below. If not, write down how you kept them from returning. (This will help all members of your group.)

2. How are you going to allow God to help you get rid of any new defects of character that you discovered in working this lesson? Be specific.

3. What are some positive things with which you can replace a defect of character? Please be as detailed as possible. This will encourage the rest of your group.

4. List some of the tools and good habits you are currently using to grow closer to God.

5. What is the biggest struggle you are dealing with today? Share how it is affecting you as well as how you plan, with God's power, to overcome it.

Prayer

Dear God, thank You for taking me this far in The Journey Continues. *Now I pray for Your help in making me entirely ready to change all my shortcomings. Give me the strength to deal with all of my character defects that I have turned over to You, and allow me to accept all the changes You want to make in me. Help me be the person that You want me to be. My heart is open. In Your Son's name I pray, amen.*

Lesson 15

Victory

Principle 5: Voluntarily submit to any and all changes God wants to make in my life and humbly ask Him to remove my character defects.

"Happy are those whose greatest desire is to do what God requires." *(Matthew 5:6)*

Step 6: We were entirely ready to have God remove all these defects of character.

"Humble yourselves before the Lord, and he will lift you up." *(James 4:10)*

Step 7: We humbly asked Him to remove all our shortcomings.

"If we confess our sins, he is faithful and just and will forgive us our sins and purify us from all unrighteousness." (1 John 1:9)

Please begin your time together by reading "The Seventh Step, Day 180" from the *Celebrate Recovery Daily Devotional.*

Since starting Celebrate Recovery, you have undoubtedly found great victory over certain areas of your life. No one is saying you're "done" or "perfect," but hopefully you are noticing some major changes. Victory can mean different things to different people. Maybe you have obtained sobriety and have found freedom in an area that previously held you captive. Maybe your reactions are changing, and you are no longer flying off the handle or responding negatively to situations. It might be that you are now able to establish clear boundaries with the people in your life.

Let's look at some ways we can identify, protect, and enjoy the victory we now have, and that is still to come.

VICTORY

V—Value small changes

One of the things that can keep us stuck in recovery is forgetting that small, steady change is the key to continued growth. We often look for overnight change—to be completely transformed all at once—instead of looking for the many small ways we are becoming different. Take the time to notice and celebrate the changes and victories God is giving you, no matter how small.

"For this very reason, make every effort to add to your faith goodness; and to goodness, knowledge; and to knowledge, self-control; and to self-control, perseverance; and to perseverance, godliness; and to godliness, mutual affection; and to mutual affection, love." (2 Peter 1:5–7)

"Not that I have already obtained all this, or have already arrived at my goal, but I press on to take hold of that for which Christ Jesus took hold of me. Brothers and sisters, I do not consider myself yet to have taken hold of it. But one thing I do: Forgetting what is behind and straining toward what is ahead, I press on toward the goal to win the prize for which God has called me heavenward in Christ Jesus." (Philippians 3:12–14)

I—Identify what needs attention next

When we first start Celebrate Recovery, we usually work on a major issue that is causing us pain. In fact, for those unsure about what changes they need to make, we often ask them to think about what is causing them the most trouble, *right now*. But once we have been in recovery for a while, it may seem harder to identify what we should work on next. Maybe we have found some freedom from the issue that brought us here, and now we wonder how to proceed further. That's why it's so important to repeat the process of a moral inventory.

"Show me your ways, Lord, teach me your paths. Guide me in your truth and teach me, for you are God my Savior, and my hope is in you all day long." (Psalm 25:4–5)

"The secret things belong to the Lord our God, but the things revealed belong to us and to our children forever, that we may follow all the words of this law." (Deuteronomy 29:29)

C—Celebrate what God has done in our lives

What do teams do after they win? They cheer! They celebrate their victory. Now that we have experienced some victory, we ought to celebrate it! When we react more positively under stress, or when we choose to pray instead of acting out, or when we notice that we are different, let's celebrate what God has done and praise Him for it!

"A cheerful heart is good medicine, but a crushed spirit dries up the bones." (Proverbs 17:22)

"Praise the Lord. Praise God in his sanctuary; praise him in his mighty heavens. Praise him for his acts of power; praise him for his surpassing greatness." (Psalm 150:1–2)

T—Tell someone else about our victory

When God gives you victory over a hurt, hang-up, or habit, He doesn't give it just to you, He gives it to all of us. We need to know the about the victory you have found. Hearing about your change, your victory, encourages the rest of us to keep going. It lets us know that God is able to heal us, too. So, find someone you can share with. And don't worry about this coming off as bragging. You won't be bragging about what you have done but about what God has done for you!

> *"But he said to me, 'My grace is sufficient for you, for my power is made perfect in weakness.' Therefore I will boast all the more gladly about my weaknesses, so that Christ's power may rest on me." (2 Corinthians 12:9)*

> *"But in your hearts revere Christ as Lord. Always be prepared to give an answer to everyone who asks you to give the reason for the hope that you have. But do this with gentleness and respect." (1 Peter 3:15)*

O — One day at a time still applies, and always will

Once we have found some victory over our hurts, hang-ups, and habits, it can become tempting to think we are done, that we are completely healed. While we may have found freedom over our addictions or compulsive thoughts, we need to remain diligent so that we don't fall back into unhealthy patterns or relapse. That's one reason why we identify ourselves as "a believer who struggles with. . . ." We are one mistake, one poor choice, away from catastrophe and so, to maintain the victory we have found, and in order to find victory in new areas, we must continue to live one day at a time.

> *"Therefore I tell you, do not worry about your life, what you will eat or drink; or about your body, what you will wear. Is not life more than food, and the body more than clothes? Look at the birds of the air; they do not sow or reap or store away in barns, and yet your heavenly Father feeds them. Are you not much more valuable than they? Can any one of you by worrying add a single hour to your life? And why do you worry about*

clothes? See how the flowers of the field grow. They do not labor or spin. Yet I tell you that not even Solomon in all his splendor was dressed like one of these. If that is how God clothes the grass of the field, which is here today and tomorrow is thrown into the fire, will he not much more clothe you—you of little faith?

"So do not worry, saying, 'What shall we eat?' or 'What shall we drink?' or 'What shall we wear?' For the pagans run after all these things, and your heavenly Father knows that you need them. But seek first his kingdom and his righteousness, and all these things will be given to you as well. Therefore do not worry about tomorrow, for tomorrow will worry about itself. Each day has enough trouble of its own." (Matthew 6:25–34)

R—Realize there are battles still to come

The battle against our hurts, hang-ups, and habits is ongoing! While we may have found some victory, we would be foolish to think there won't be battles ahead. This is why it's so important to set aside daily time with God to prepare us for the days when we struggle.

"Put on the full armor of God, so that you can take your stand against the devil's schemes. For our struggle is not against flesh and blood, but against the rulers, against the authorities, against the powers of this dark world and against the spiritual forces of evil in the heavenly realms. Therefore put on the full armor of God, so that when the day of evil comes, you may be able to stand your ground, and after you have done everything, to stand. Stand firm then, with the belt of truth buckled around your waist, with the breastplate of righteousness in place, and with your feet fitted with the readiness that comes from the gospel of peace. In addition to all this, take up the shield of faith, with which you can extinguish all the flaming arrows of the evil one. Take the helmet of salvation and the sword of the Spirit, which is the word of God." (Ephesians 6:11–17)

Y—You are not alone

It's tempting sometimes to feel isolated and alone. Even now, you may feel as if no one has ever gone through what you're going through. But look around your group. The people in your group are there for you. It's vital that you remain in communication with your sponsor, your accountability partner/team, and the other members of your group. When things feel too hard or when you feel like giving up, your team can surround you and hold you up! They can encourage you and keep you on track. And you can do the same for them!

> *"Therefore, since we are surrounded by such a great cloud of witnesses, let us throw off everything that hinders and the sin that so easily entangles. And let us run with perseverance the race marked out for us." (Hebrews 12:1)*

Questions for Reflection and Discussion

1. What is a major victory you have experienced in Celebrate Recovery? Share it with your group.

2. What small changes have you noticed? How have you celebrated them in the past?

3. What hurt, hang-up, or habit needs your attention next?

4. How are you celebrating what God has done for you through Celebrate Recovery? And if you've failed to celebrate the victories He has given you in the past, why do you think that is so?

5. Who can you tell about the victories you have experienced?

6. How are you still living one day at a time?

7. How do you daily put on the "armor of God"? What piece of the armor do you feel like you most need today? Why?

8. What do you do when you start to feel isolated and alone?

9. What steps can you take to help others know they are not alone?

Prayer

Father, thank You for all of the victories, big and small, You have given me through Celebrate Recovery. Thank You for all of the ways I am different today. I ask You to help me see all of the ways I have changed and to trust You with the next areas You want me to work on. I can't praise You enough for what You've done. Help me find others to encourage with the victory You have given me. Amen.

Lesson 16

Amends

Principle 6: Evaluate all my relationships. Offer forgiveness to those who have hurt me and make amends for harm I've done to others, except when to do so would harm them or others.

"Happy are the merciful." (Matthew 5:7)

"Happy are the peacemakers." (Matthew 5:9)

Step 8: We made a list of all persons we had harmed and became willing to make amends to them all.

"Do to others as you would have them do to you." (Luke 6:31)

Please begin your time together by reading "The Eight Step, Day 210" from the *Celebrate Recovery Daily Devotional.*

Principle 6 is all about making amends. "Forgive me as I learn to forgive" sums it up pretty well.

Before we got to this principle in *The Journey Begins*, we started doing repair work on the personal side of our lives. We did this by admitting our powerlessness, turning our lives and wills over to God's care, doing our moral inventory, sharing our sins or wrongs with another, and admitting our shortcomings and asking God to remove them. But then we began to do some repair work on the relational side of our lives.

We learned that making amends is not about our past so much as it is about our future. Before we could have the healthy relationships that we desired, we needed to clean out the guilt, shame, and pain that has caused many of our past relationships to fail.

Step 8 tells us, it is time to "make a list of persons we have harmed and become willing to make amends to them all." At this point, we are only looking for the willingness to do so, to simply identify those to whom we need to make amends or offer forgiveness.

Important Note: Find the "Amends List" worksheet on page 43 of Participant's Guide 2 of *The Journey Begins* step study. Make sure you completed making your amends to all the people on your most recent list. If not, start there. Then use the new Principle 6 Worksheet found in this lesson on page 51 and ask God to show you all the outstanding and new people to whom you owe an amends since you completed *The Journey Begins.*

In Column 1 of your inventory that you completed in *The Journey Continues* (your newest one), you will find the list of people you need to forgive. These are the people who have hurt you. In Column 5, you will find the list of people to whom you owe amends. Transfer these names to the Principle 6 Worksheet.

Let's look at the AMENDS acrostic that will answer these three questions:

How do I make amends the way God tells us to?

Who do I need to make new amends to?

Which amends were incomplete or not done at all when I did this lesson in *The Journey Begins*?

AMENDS

A—Admit the hurt and the harm

We need to see the hurtful act for the "true harm" we did to them. We shouldn't minimize or exaggerate the harm we caused.

"They dress the wound of my people as though it were not serious. 'Peace, peace,' they say, when there is no peace." (Jeremiah 6:14)

M—Make a list

Add any new or incomplete amends that we have to make. It's very important to write them down. We can't rely on memory.

"I think it is right to refresh your memory as long as I live in the tent of this body." (2 Peter 1:13)

E—Encourage one another

We do not have to do all of this on our own. It's so important to share the amends we are planning to make with our accountability partner/team or sponsor before making the actual amends to the person. Remember Principle 6: "Evaluate all my relationships. Offer forgiveness to those who have hurt me and make amends for harm I've done to others, *except when to do so would harm them or others.*"

"Test me, Lord, and try me, examine my heart and my mind." (Psalm 26:2)

"But encourage one another daily, as long as it is called 'Today,' so that none of you may be hardened by sin's deceitfulness." (Hebrews 3:13)

N—Not just for those we hurt

Making our amends, admitting our wrongs, sets us free. We no longer have to carry around the guilt of the things we have done. While we can't undo anything, we can rest knowing we are doing our part to make our relationships healthy.

"Do to others as you would have them do to you." (Luke 6:31)

D—Do it at the right time

Before contacting the person to make amends, pray. Ask God for His perfect timing.

"Humble yourselves, therefore, under God's mighty hand, that he may lift you up in due time." (1 Peter 5:6)

"A person finds joy in giving an apt reply—and how good is a timely word!" (Proverbs 15:23)

S—Start living all the promises of God—again

Celebrate that our loads have been lightened!

"Come to me, all you who are weary and burdened, and I will give you rest. Take my yoke upon you and learn from me, for I am gentle and humble in heart, and you will find rest for your souls. For my yoke is easy and my burden is light." (Matthew 11:28–30)

"The Lord is trustworthy in all he promises and faithful in all he does." (Psalm 145:13)

Principle 6 Worksheet

Principle 6: Evaluate all my relationships. Offer forgiveness to those who have hurt me and make amends for harm I've done to others when possible, except when to do so would harm them or others.

"Happy are the merciful. . . . Happy are the peacemakers."
(Matthew 5:7, 9)

Who do I need to give amends to? Name and Reason	Who do I need to forgive? Name and Reason

Questions for Reflection and Discussion

1. Why is it so important for you to not minimize or exaggerate the harm you caused when you make your amends?

2. Which do you typically do: minimize or exaggerate? Why?

3. Who are the first people you included on your Principle 6 Worksheet that you will start making your amends to? List three.

4. Principle 6 says, "Evaluate all my relationships. Offer forgiveness to those who have hurt me and *make amends for harm I've done to others, except when to do so would harm them or others.*" Describe how you

interpret the italicized part of Principle 6. Have you ever used it as an excuse to not make amends? Why?

5. How does making your amends help set you free?

6. How do you determine when it is the right time to make an amends?

7. How do you handle it when it someone rejects your amends?

8. How can you encourage your accountability partner/team to make the amends they need to make?

9. How do you celebrate when you make an amends and it is accepted by the person you made it to?

Prayer

Dear God, I pray for willingness — willingness to evaluate all my past and current relationships. Please show me the people I have hurt, and help me become willing to offer my amends to them. Also, God, give me Your strength to become willing to offer forgiveness to those who have hurt me. I pray for Your perfect timing for taking the action that Principle 6 calls for. I ask all these things in Your Son's name, amen.

Lesson 17

Forgiveness

Principle 6: Evaluate all my relationships. Offer forgiveness to those who have hurt me and make amends for harm I've done to others when possible, except when to do so would harm them or others.

"Happy are the merciful." (Matthew 5:7)

"Happy are the peacemakers." (Matthew 5:9)

Step 8: We made a list of all the persons we had harmed and became willing to make amends to them all.

"Do to others as you would have them do to you." (Luke 6:31)

Step 9: We made direct amends to such people whenever possible, except when to do so would injure them or others.

"Therefore, if you are offering your gift at the altar and there remember that your brother or sister has something against you, leave your gift there in front of the altar. First go and be reconciled to them; then come and offer your gift." (Matthew 5:23–24)

Please begin your time together by reading "Forgiving Others, Day 65" from the *Celebrate Recovery Daily Devotional.*

In Lesson 17 of *The Journey Begins*, we looked at the three different kinds of forgiveness: God's forgiveness toward us, our need to forgive others who have hurt us, and the need to forgive ourselves for the things we have done. At first, it may have been difficult to accept or extend one or more of these areas of forgiveness. But now that we've been in recovery a while, it is likely that we have experienced both extending and being shown forgiveness, and have observed firsthand how freeing it is to let go of our resentments, anger, fears, and shame. We have done a moral inventory at least twice (once in *The Journey Begins* and now in *The Journey Continues*) and have seen many of the names from our original inventory no longer show up on our newest one.

However, there may still be some people we have yet to forgive. They may have hurt us deeply, or they may have hurt us recently. Let's look at three reasons to forgive those who have hurt us:

Reason 1: Jesus tells us to forgive others.

Reason 2: We need forgiveness from others.

Reason 3: Trust cannot be earned until forgiveness is given.

Reason 1: Jesus tells us to forgive others.

In Principle 3, we make the decision to turn our lives and our wills over to Jesus Christ. As a result, we exchange our way of doing things for His. When we turn our wills over to Jesus, we are telling Him that we will do what He tells us to. We agree that He knows best for us, and we accept that His ways will be better than our own. And Jesus tells us repeatedly to forgive those who have hurt us.

"Then Peter came to Jesus and asked, 'Lord, how many times shall I forgive my brother or sister who sins against me? Up to seven times?' Jesus answered, 'I tell you, not seven times, but seventy-seven times.'" (Matthew 18:21–22)

"Forgive us our sins, for we also forgive everyone who sins against us. And lead us not into temptation." (Luke 11:4)

Reason 2: We need forgiveness from others.

Remember that "*all* have sinned and fall short of the glory of God" (Romans 3:23), which means while we have been hurt by people, we have also hurt people. We need to model for others how we would like to be treated. If we ourselves have unforgiving hearts, when others ask us for forgiveness, we will be met with a similar attitude. Because we will need forgiveness, we ought to extend forgiveness, whether or not the other person asks for it or deserves it.

"Be kind and compassionate to one another, forgiving each other, just as in Christ God forgave you." (Ephesians 4:32)

Reason 3: Trust cannot be earned until forgiveness is given.

Forgiveness and trust are not the same thing. When someone hurts us, or when we hurt other people, rebuilding trust takes time and effort. It takes progressive changes in actions and attitudes. Regaining trust will take time. Some people who have hurt us may never deserve or earn our trust—they might be unsafe for us to be around. But look back at Reason 1 again. Jesus doesn't tell us to forgive people who deserve it, but to forgive them anyway.

However, if you want to do your part in restoring relationships, if trust is going to be rebuilt, it starts with forgiving the person who harmed you. You may never forget what they did to you, but you will need to let go of it and forgive them to move forward. This is different from denial, because you aren't pretending nothing happened, but you are choosing to let it go and start the process of rebuilding trust.

"If it is possible, as far as it depends on you, live at peace with everyone." (Romans 12:18)

"Bear with each other and forgive one another if any of you has a grievance against someone. Forgive as the Lord forgave you." (Colossians 3:13)

Forgiveness can be hard, but it is essential to your growth. As you think about those whom you need to forgive, ask yourself if holding onto the pain of the past is helping you or hurting you. Remember that forgiveness is often an attitude of the heart. If the person you need to forgive is not be safe for you to talk to directly, you may choose to write a letter you never intend to send or use the "empty chair" method. This is where you offer your forgiveness, out loud, to a chair that represents the person you are forgiving. But whenever possible, offering forgiveness needs to be done face-to-face. These other methods should be reserved only for people who are unsafe for you or who are still hurting you. Talk to your sponsor and accountability partners and ask for guidance and prayer on how to proceed.

Also, remember that forgiving the person who has hurt you does not make what they did acceptable. It does not let them off the hook. Instead, it gives you the freedom to finally let go of the pain they caused you.

Important Note: Remember to add the names found in Column 1 of your spiritual inventory to the "Who do I need to forgive" section of the Principle 6 Worksheet on page 51. As you complete this lesson, add any additional names as God reveals them to you. Don't forget to reference your spiritual inventory from *The Journey Begins* as well, to see if there is anyone whom that list that you have yet to forgive.

(For additional information on forgiveness, refer to pages 168–175 of *Life's Healing Choices.*)

Questions for Reflection and Discussion

1. Who do you need to forgive today? Why? What has stopped you in the past from forgiving them?

2. Share about a time you forgave someone and how it affected your recovery.

3. Are there people you need to forgive who are unsafe for you to forgive face-to-face? If so, why and how will you forgive them?

4. Which of the three reasons for forgiving others is most important to you right now? Why?

5. Is there anyone from a previous moral inventory you have yet to forgive? List them here. Why do you think you were, or are still, unwilling to forgive them?

6. How does trust differ from forgiveness in your mind?

7. In what ways are you being controlled by your unwillingness to forgive someone else?

8. What does "living at peace with everyone" mean to you?

9. Have you ever needed forgiveness from someone you were unwilling to forgive?

Prayer

Heavenly Father, please help me forgive the people in my life who have hurt me. I know that You have forgiven me of so much. Help me let go of the pain of the past and be free of the hurt done to me. If possible, help me do my part to make broken relationships healthy again. Amen.

Lesson 18

Grace

Principle 6: Evaluate all my relationships. Offer forgiveness to those who have hurt me and make amends for harm I've done to others, except when to do so would harm them or others.

"Happy are the merciful." (Matthew 5:6)

"Happy are the peacemakers." (Matthew 5:9)

Step 9: Made direct amends to such people whenever possible, except when to do so would injure them or others.

"Therefore, if you are offering your gift at the altar and there remember that your brother or sister has something against you, leave your gift there in front of the altar. First go and be reconciled to them; then come and offer your gift." (Matthew 5:23–24)

Please begin your time together by reading "The Ninth Step, Day 240" from the *Celebrate Recovery Daily Devotional.*

This is the last lesson on Principle 6. We have revisited how to evaluate all our relationships, offer forgiveness to those who have hurt us, and make amends for the harm that we have done to others, when possible, without expecting anything back.

As we grow closer to Jesus and as we grow in our recovery, we want to follow His guidance and directions. As we get to know Him better, we want to model His teachings and model His ways. We want to become more like Him. Honestly, if we are going to implement Principle 6 to the best of our ability, we need to continue to learn to model God's grace.

One of the key verses of Celebrate Recovery is 2 Corinthians 12:9–10, "But he said to me, 'My grace is sufficient for you, for my power is made perfect in weakness.' Therefore I will boast all the more gladly about my weaknesses, so that Christ's power may rest on me. That is why, for Christ's sake, I delight in weaknesses, in insults, in hardships, in persecutions, in difficulties. For when I am weak, then I am strong."

Now that we have almost completed *The Journey Continues*, it's important that we commit yet another verse to memory:

"However, I consider my life worth nothing to me; my only aim is to finish the race and complete the task the Lord Jesus has given me—the task of testifying to the good news of God's grace." (Acts 20:24)

> Celebrate Recovery is built on and centered in Christ's grace and love for each of us. As you know, *The Journey Continues* contains new acrostics and new verses. However, we hope you will extend us *your* grace as we determined we couldn't improve on the original GRACE acrostic found in lesson 18 of *The Journey Begins.*

Let's look at the acrostic: GRACE.

GRACE

G—God's gift

Grace cannot be bought. It is freely given by God to you and me. When we offer (give) our amends and expect nothing back, that's a gift from us to those whom we have hurt.

"For all have sinned and fall short of the glory of God, and all are justified freely by his grace through the redemption that came by Christ Jesus." (Romans 3:23–24)

"Therefore, with minds that are alert and fully sober, set your hope on the grace to be brought to you when Jesus Christ is revealed at his coming." (1 Peter 1:13)

R—Received by our faith

No matter how hard we may work, we cannot earn our way into heaven. Only by professing our faith in Jesus Christ as our Lord and Savior can we experience His grace and have eternal life.

"For it is by grace you have been saved, through faith—and this not from yourselves, it is the gift of God—not by works, so that no one can boast." (Ephesians 2:8–9)

"And be found in him, not having a righteousness of my own that comes from the law, but that which is through faith in Christ—the righteousness that comes from God on the basis of faith." (Philippians 3:9)

A—Accepted by God's love

> *I don't know about you, but I know that I do not deserve God's love. But the good news is He accepts me in spite of myself! He sees all my failures and loves me anyway. And the same goes for you.*
>
> —John Baker

"But because of his great love for us, God, who is rich in mercy, made us alive with Christ even when we were dead in transgressions—it is by grace you have been saved." (Ephesians 2:4–5)

"Let us then approach God's throne of grace with confidence, so that we may receive mercy and find grace to help us in our time of need." (Hebrews 4:16)

C—Christ paid the price

Jesus died on the cross so that all our sins, all our wrongs, are forgiven. He paid the price, sacrificed Himself for you and me so that we may be with Him forever.

"In him we have redemption through his blood, the forgiveness of sins, in accordance with the riches of God's grace." (Ephesians 1:7)

"I do not set aside the grace of God, for if righteousness could be gained through the law, Christ died for nothing!" (Galatians 2:21)

E—Everlasting gift

Once you have accepted Jesus Christ as your Savior and Lord, God's gift of grace is forever.

"May our Lord Jesus Christ himself and God our Father, who loved us and by his grace gave us eternal encouragement and good hope, encourage your hearts and strengthen you in every good deed and word." (2 Thessalonians 2:16–17)

"All over the world this gospel is bearing fruit and growing, just as it has been doing among you since the day you heard it and understood God's grace in all its truth." (Colossians 1:6)

> *Christ did not suffer and die to offer cheap grace. Jesus did not willingly go to the cross so we could have an easy life or offer a faith built on easy-believism. As someone said, "Salvation is free, but not cheap." It cost Jesus His life.*
>
> —Billy Graham

Questions for Reflection and Discussion

1. Grace is God's gift. Four words that change everything. What does that statement mean to you?

2. Describe how different your life would be if you had to earn God's grace.

3. John Baker said, "I don't know about you, but I know that I do not deserve God's love. But the good news is He accepts me in spite of myself! He sees all my failures and loves me anyway. And the same goes for you." How does that statement relate to your life? Be specific.

4. Put into words how knowing that Jesus died for you makes you feel. Also, how has it changed your daily life?

Prayer

God, we stand before You as a product of Your grace. Everyone here in this group who has asked Christ into their lives is also a product of Your love. As we model Your grace, we are able to do the work that Principle 6 requires.

We close with Colossians 1:6: "All over the world this gospel is bearing fruit and growing, just as it has been doing among [us] since the day [we] heard it and understood God's grace in all its truth."

Amen.

Afterword

Before you jump into the last book of *The Journey Continues*, take a minute to think about all of the things you have experienced so far. You have done some amazing work! It can be so tempting to just keep moving and not stop to reflect on what God has done. So take just a few minutes and thank God for all He has done for you thus far.

If you have seen new areas in which to apply the principles of recovery, thank Him for revealing them to you.

If you have been reminded to do your part in restoring a relationship, ask Him for the power to do the next right thing.

If you have found others who have supported you, or as you have been supporting other people, thank Him for placing these people in your life.

If you have found freedom over any new or older hurts, hang-ups, or habits, thank Him for working in your life and setting you free.

Now, get ready for Participant's Guide 8, *Living Out the Message of Christ!*

ALSO AVAILABLE

CELEBRATE RECOVERY 30 ANNIVERSARY

Celebrate Recovery®

365 DAILY DEVOTIONAL

This daily devotional is specially designed to complement the Celebrate Recovery® program. It features 366 brief original readings, each a powerful reminder of God's goodness, grace, and redemption and an inspiration to anyone struggling with old hurts, habits, and hang-ups. The *Celebrate Recovery 365 Daily Devotional* will encourage everyone who is on the road to recovery.

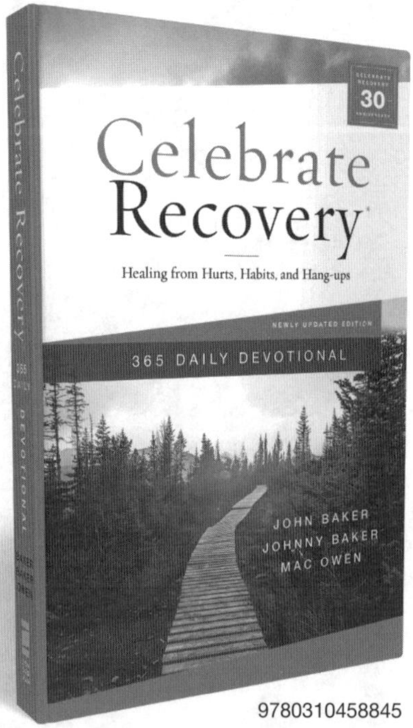

9780310458845

Available now at your favorite bookstore.

ZONDERVAN®

ALSO AVAILABLE

CELEBRATE RECOVERY 30 ANNIVERSARY

Celebrate Recovery®

LEADER'S KIT

For over 30 years, Celebrate Recovery® has helped the church fulfill its role as Christ's healing agent. Since 1991, millions of people have participated in the Celebrate Recovery programs offered at more than 35,000 churches, prisons, and rescue missions in 21 different languages. Developed by John Baker and Rick Warren of Saddleback Church, Celebrate Recovery draws from the Beatitudes to help people overcome their hurts, hang-ups,and habits. Rather than setting up an isolated recovery community, this powerful program helps participants and their churches come together and discover new levels of care, acceptance, trust, and grace.

Leader's Kit: 9780310131601

The 30th anniversary leader's kit includes:

- 1 *Celebrate Recovery Leader's Guide*
- 1 each of *The Journey Begins* participant's guides #1-4
- 1 each of *The Journey Continues* participant's guides #5-8
- 1 Leader's Resource USB stick with 25 editable lessons from *The Journey Begins* curriculum, three videos featuring John Baker, Johnny Baker, and Rick Warren, sermon transcripts, and MP3 sermons.
- 1 *NIV Celebrate Recovery Study Bible*, Comfort Print® edition
- 1 copy of *Your First Step to Celebrate Recovery*
- 1 copy of *Celebrate Recovery 28 Devotions*

Available now at your favorite bookstore.

ZONDERVAN®